This book belongs to:

....

Ella Bop
A Coloring Book For New Parents

© 2013 Ella Bop
Outside The Lines Press

www.outsidethelinespress.com

ALL RIGHTS RESERVED

Pediatricians recommend starting your child on solid food at approximately 6 months

"Honey, I think that food is a little *too* solid."

Reading to your children is strongly correlated with future academic success*

*But don't go overboard

For some women, getting a newborn to latch
during breastfeeding can be challenging

"My friend Alice said that a football hold is the
ideal breastfeeding position, but I don't get it."

Choosing your baby's name is an important decision that sometimes requires months of thought and deliberation

"So what name should I put on the certificate ma'am?"

"Hold on a sec. OK honey, heads it's Katniss, tails it's Galadriel!"

Children usually contract a number of common childhood illnesses before the age of four

"What's wrong with your son???"

"Cradle cap, chicken pox, roseola, head lice, impetigo, conjunctivitis. You name it. Just avert your eyes."

Your baby has an ear infection. Match the image of the person providing unsolicited advice with their suggestion for what needs to be done.

Your holistic neighbor

"Take him to the Emergency Room!"

Your hypochondriacal cousin

"Pour a cup of olive oil in his ear, wrap him in a wool blanket and leave him outside in the fresh air for 6 hours."

Your husband

"Put some ground algae and Echinacea root in a solution of raw goat's milk and soy extract, and rub it on his chest."

"Give him a paracetamol and the iPad!"

Your great-aunt Muriel

Color the different types of baby poop!

Meconium
(black)

Breastfed poop
(green)

Formula-fed poop
(tan, brown)

solid-food poop
(dark brown, orange for the
partially digested carrots)

New parents have had their horizons expanded, leading to a much richer variety of conversation topics

BEFORE KIDS

AFTER KIDS

"But the current economic crisis has been precipitated by a systemic failure of the global regulatory framework; it's not just a liquidity issue. Have you read Krugman's op-ed piece in the Wall Street Journal yet?"

"Bradley made his first poo-poo in the potty this morning! It was such a big poo-poo! I bet you've never seen a poo-poo this big before! I took a picture of it - do you want to see it?"

New parents are often unnecessarily worried about exposing their newborns to germs

"She's adorable! Can I hold her?"

"Sure! Just one sec... Honey, do we have a hazmat suit in Brian's size?"

Resuming normal social activities after the birth of your baby takes time

"It's great to finally see you out of the house! Wait... what's that smell? Does he need a change?"

"No that's me; I haven't had time to shower since last January."

New Parents Word Find

```
Y  A  I  G  X  B  U  R  P  I  N  G  I  I  J
Q  M  S  Q  T  X  Z  C  Y  F  D  K  A  N  P
W  L  Q  L  X  H  Y  K  I  G  D  R  O  O  L
E  T  L  Z  S  R  N  S  C  L  I  M  V  I  Q
G  P  Q  Q  G  I  O  W  H  A  O  R  U  T  K
R  M  M  O  B  L  T  F  X  O  Q  C  Y  A  N
A  B  F  J  I  G  N  I  H  T  E  E  T  V  C
X  R  F  D  C  L  G  Q  T  E  Y  M  K  I  M
F  S  S  A  V  M  T  Y  R  O  H  Q  F  R  B
Y  N  J  P  E  E  L  S  S  I  A  C  H  P  V
I  V  S  L  A  C  T  A  T  I  O  N  T  E  H
F  L  R  I  D  I  H  S  A  R  R  W  W  D  E
E  V  S  H  R  O  Z  U  R  C  P  M  T  W  L
E  T  R  O  D  S  T  Y  P  L  C  E  M  M  O
E  Z  W  T  H  T  Z  H  I  L  H  L  T  R  K
```

colic   solids
sleep   otitis
teething   MMR
drool   binky
lactation   burping
rash

It is important for new parents to keep the romance alive after the arrival of a newborn. Take time to be with each other.

There is an inverse relationship between the size of a child, and the amount of luggage you will need to take with you when going on vacation

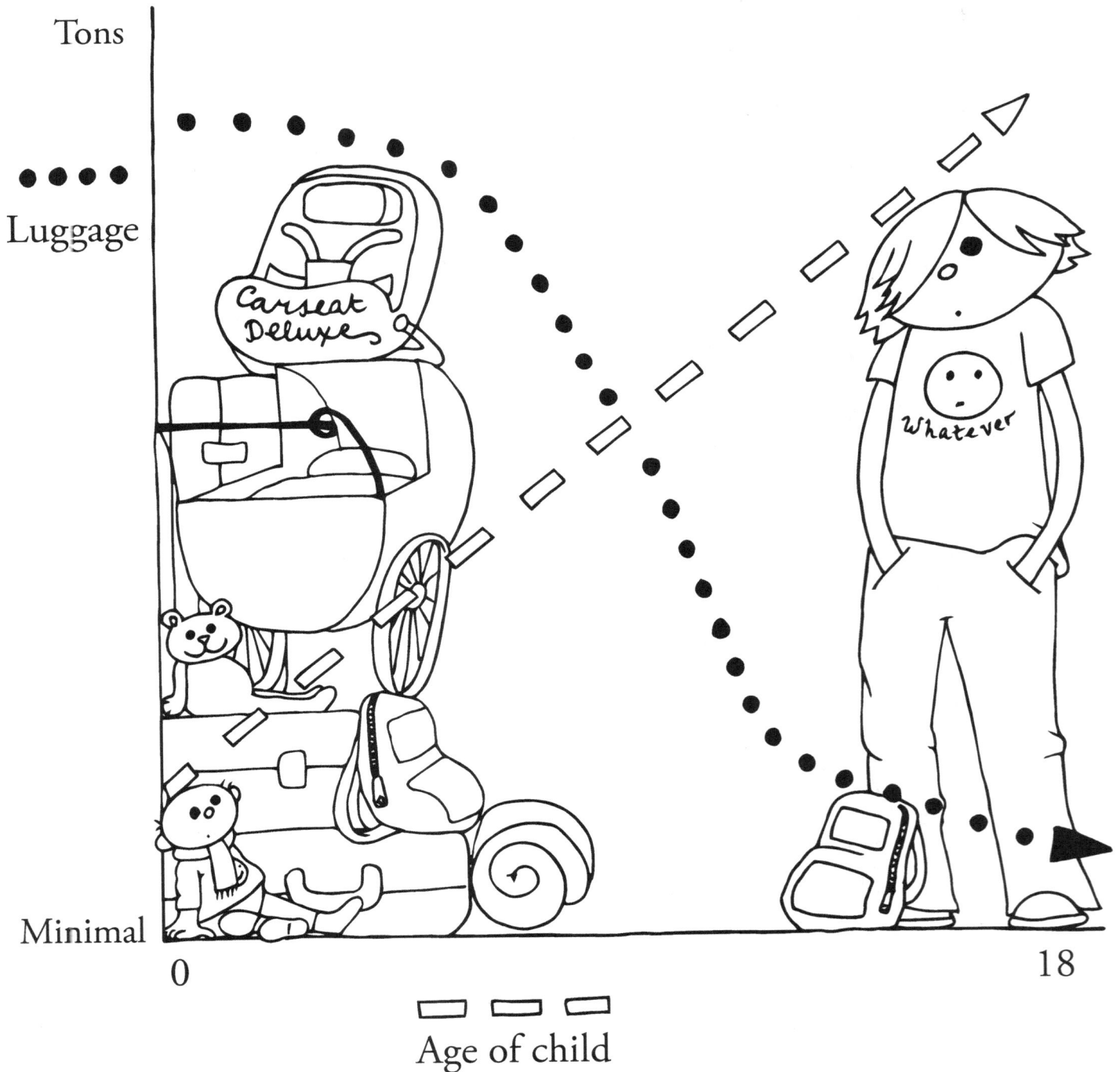

Tons

Luggage

Carseat Deluxe

Whatever

Minimal

0

18

Age of child

Caring for a screaming baby on an airplane is a rite of passage for many new parents

Live vicariously through your baby by dressing him/ her up in an adorable little outfit that symbolizes the remnants of your broken dreams!

DIPLOMA

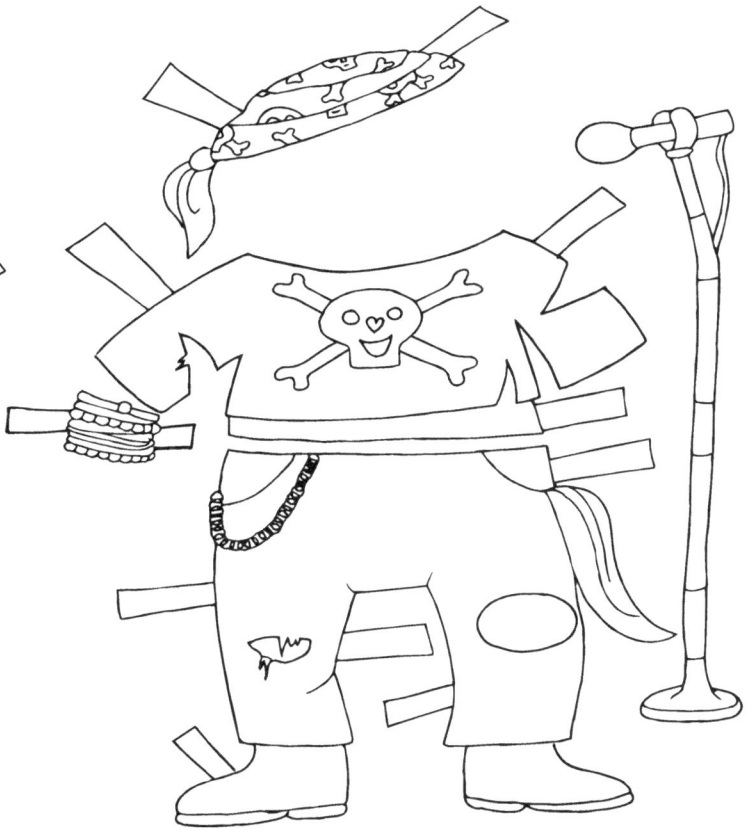

Young children have a propensity for putting things in their mouths, which is a normal part of oral and sensory-motor development

"Honey, have you seen my keys?"

Uh-oh! Your baby just shoved a Lego up his nose. Connect the dots to see dad's solution for how to extract it!

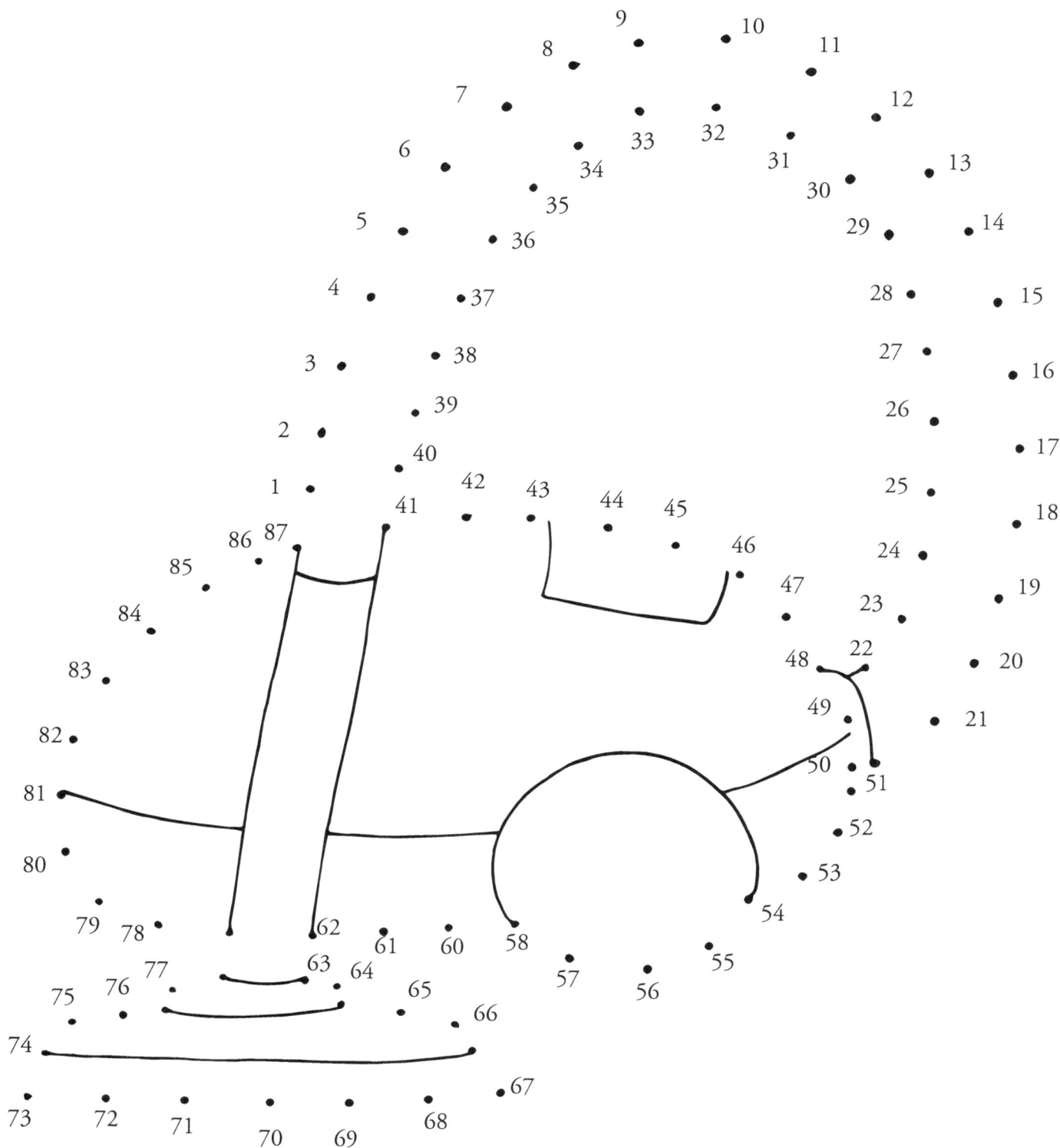

It is not always easy to ascertain the gender of an infant at first glance

"He's adorable, what's his name?"

"**_Her_** name is Jennifer. Honey, can you grab a pink bow or pink hat or something pink please??"

Overseeing your child's linguistic development is one of the greatest privileges of parenthood

"I simply cannot wait until she starts talking!"

"Will this kid ever stop talking???"

It's not always easy to determine the cause of your baby's crying

"I give up! What's wrong with him? Is he hungry? Too cold? Too hot? Is he overtired? Is he wet? Is he sick? Does he have a fever? Is he teething? "

"You're sitting on his teddy bear."

A lullaby sung by a loving parent will sooth the fussiest of babies

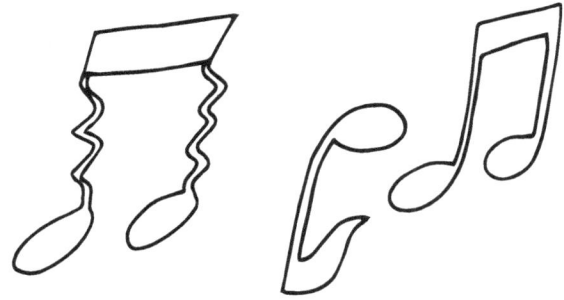

"Stop! Collaborate and listen. Ice is back with a brand new edition!"

Baby-proofing the home is vital to keeping your little tyke safe as he begins to explore his environment

Young children have not yet developed food
preferences or a sophisticated palette, and will
eat nearly any food they encounter

New parents can forget about getting a good night's sleep

2:42AM feeding

3:17AM diaper change

4:35AM crying for no reason

3:58AM baby is too warm

4:08AM baby is too cold

5:17AM baby has cramps

Watching a baby sleep is one of the most satisfying things in the world

"I think we should wake him up for his 3:00 feeding."

"If you wake that baby up, we are getting a divorce."

Totally worth it

For more from the *Coloring Books for Adults series* from Outside The Lines Press, visit:

www.outsidethelinespress.com

Other titles in this series include:

A Coloring Book for Pregnant Ladies

Coming soon:

A Coloring Book for Brides
A Coloring Book for Bridesmaids
A Coloring Book for Newlyweds
A Coloring Book for Dog Lovers
A Coloring Book for Cat Lovers
A Coloring Book for 30 Somethings